FISHING VIRGINIA'S HIGHLANDS

AN ANGLER'S GUIDE

Fishing Virginia's Highlands

M. W. Smith

University of Virginia Press

CHARLOTTESVILLE AND LONDON

University of Virginia Press

© 2007 by the Rector and Visitors of the University of Virginia

Printed in the United States of America on acid-free paper

First published 2007

9 8 7 6 5 4 3 2 1

LIBRARY OF CONGRESS CATALOGING-IN-PUBLICATION DATA

Smith, M. W. (Michael W.), 1963–

   Fishing Virginia's highlands : an angler's guide / M.W. Smith.

      p.   cm.

   ISBN 978-0-8139-2657-5 (pbk. : alk. paper)

   1. Fishing—Virginia—Guidebooks. 2. Virginia—Guidebooks. I. Title.

SH557.S65 2007

799.1209755—dc22

                                                        2007009400

All photographs by King Montgomery,

used courtesy of the photographer

Maps by Chris Harrison

To my daughter, Brook

I am haunted by waters.

—NORMAN MACLEAN,
A RIVER RUNS THROUGH IT

Contents

Preface

Welcome to *Fishing Virginia's Highlands: An Angler's Guide.* This book covers two remote regions of the state that share many geographic characteristics, most notably their designations as "highlands." The Alleghany Highlands to the north includes Alleghany, Bath, and Rockbridge counties (which border West Virginia), while farther southwest, the Blue Ridge/Grayson Highlands and the surrounding Mount Rogers National Recreation Area take in Grayson, Smyth, and Washington counties (which border North Carolina and Tennessee, respectively). Mount Rogers, in Grayson County, boasts the highest elevation in the state. Besides scenic overlooks, Grayson Highlands State Park offers camping, fishing, horseback riding, hiking, nature trails, and bird watching. Alleghany Highlands, renowned for its warm springs, is home to world-famous spas, including the Homestead in Bath County. Virginia's Highlands are rich in angling lore, and their secluded lakes and rivers offer some of the best trout and smallmouth fishing found anywhere in the state. Whether you are new to the Virginia or a longtime resident, novice fisher or pro, this book will provide you with the information you need to enjoy the angling opportunities in these areas and to catch more fish from their waters.

I begin, in chapter 1, by discussing fish species common to the streams of these two regions. These include tiny native trout, feisty smallmouth bass, and elusive walleye. Chapter 2 covers, in detail and by county, many of the stocked trout streams listed by the Virginia Department of Game and Inland Fisheries (VDGIF). I offer suggestions on where and how to fish these varied streams, including both spinning and fly-fishing tactics and techniques. This chapter also addresses wild trout fishing in the Mount Rogers National Recreation Area and Grayson Highlands State Park.

Chapter 3 encompasses fishing on Lake Moomaw and the Maury River in the Alleghany Highlands. Both Lake Moomaw and the Maury River are well known for their excellent smallmouth bass fishing, but trout are also present. General instruction on how to access these waters, as well as angling strategies (including winter fishing tactics) and contact information for various services and facilities, are provided.

Chapter 4 offers detailed information on fishing South Holston Lake and the Holston River in the Blue Ridge/Grayson Highlands, with particular attention to float trips on the North Fork below Saltville. South Holston Lake has a renowned walleye and smallmouth fishery. The North Fork of the Holston River is well known for its excellent smallmouth angling, while the South Fork offers superb trout fishing. Entry and exit points for floats on the North

Fork are discussed, together with useful tips about how to negotiate its rapids. I also review techniques for fishing the river during the winter and spring months when conditions become extreme.

To supplement these particulars, you'll find a comprehensive map of the regions' streams, notes on specific fishing locations keyed to maps in DeLorme's *Virginia Atlas and Gazetteer* (6th edition), and an appendix that lists local guide services, tackle shops, camping sites, parks, and the like. In short, this book will tell you where, when, why, and how you will catch more fish in Virginia's Highlands.

Safety must be your foremost concern when floating streams. Local canoe liveries (see the appendix, pp. 77–80) can provide you with advice concerning river condition and water hazards that may require portage, as well as necessary equipment and flotation devices. The following is the list of normal stream classifications for rating rapids that are used in trip descriptions throughout this book. If the temperature is below 50°F, or the trip extends through wilderness areas, the river should be considered one class more difficult than normal.

CLASS I: Slow-moving water with small waves and few obstructions. Easy rescue.

CLASS II: Moderate rapids with waves less than three feet high and wide channels that are obvious without scouting. Some maneuvering required. Rescue level of difficulty low.

CLASS III: Formidable rapids with high, irregular waves, often capable of swamping a canoe. Narrow passages that require complex maneuvering and scouting. Rescue difficulty high.

CLASS IV: Long, difficult rapids with constricted passages that often require precise maneuvering in turbulent waters. Waves capable of swamping an open canoe. Scouting from shore a necessity, and conditions make rescue extremely difficult.

CLASS V: Dangerous and violent rapids with highly congested routes that should always be scouted from shore. Not for open canoes. Rescue conditions hazardous, with significant danger to life.

CLASS VI: Difficulties of Class V carried to the extreme of navigability, making rescue nearly impossible. For teams of expert rafters only.

Acknowledgments

Thanks first to all those who spent time on the water with me: John Kemp, Captain Forest Pressnell (aka the Outdoor Sportsman), Sterling Herbst, and Dan Mosser, as well as others from the regions who graciously shared their knowledge of the areas, including Barry Loupe, Frank Cox, Pete Messner, J. R. Bowling, and the great folks—Dan and Emily—at Twin River Outfitters. I wish once more to thank my wife, Beth, who not only fishes with me at times, but also indexes my books, and to express my gratitude to everyone at the University of Virginia Press who makes this series possible.

Fish Species Common to Virginia's Highlands

There are numerous species of fish in the lakes and streams of the highland regions. The following is a list of the more popular types of game fish you are likely to encounter.

Largemouth Bass

(Commonly called black bass.) The largemouth is dark greenish in color on top with a white belly. A series of black splotches extend laterally along its side forming a horizontal line to its tail. It has a large mouth, with an upper jaw that extends from the corner of the mouth to the rear of the eyes. The dorsal fin is deeply notched. Citation size in Virginia is 8 pounds or 22 inches. Largemouth bass are found in local ponds, lakes, and streams, including a very healthy population in both Lake Moomaw and South Holston Lake. Look for them in the coves and creek mouths where submerged vegetation, stumps, and logs are located. These fish are opportunistic feeders and will eat other fish, crayfish, snakes, frogs, and terrestrial insects. Spawning usually takes place from late April to early June.

The best artificial lures include plastic worms, jigs, crankbaits, jerk-baits, spinnerbaits, and topwater varieties.

Rock Bass

(Also know as redeye.) This fish is a member of the sunfish family and rarely weighs more than 1 pound. It has a short stout body and a large mouth. Its back is green and sides can be somewhat golden colored, and each scale has a central black spot. Dark spots on the lower body form small stripes. This species is commonly caught by smallmouth anglers, who recognize its tendency to provide a fero-cious strike with little fight to follow. Citation size in Virginia is 1 pound or 12 inches. Rock bass can be found in almost any stream with rocks and ledges in the highlands. They eat all sorts of small aquatic and terrestrial life, including crayfish, minnows, and insects, and usually spawn during the same period as the black bass. The best artificial lures include jigs and spinners.

Smallmouth Bass

(Also called bronzeback and smallie.) You can identify smallmouth by their coppery-brown color and greenish sides with dark vertical bars. Three dark bars radiate from the cheek across the gill cover, and the upper jaw does not extend as far back as a largemouth's. Ci-tation size in Virginia is 5 pounds or 20 inches. Smallies prefer cool clear water and bedrock ledges, which is why both Lake Moomaw and South Holston Lake are two of the top impoundments in the state for smallmouth bass fishing, and outstanding river fisheries are found in the Maury and the North Fork of the Holston. Crayfish, madtoms, hellgrammites, minnows, and aquatic insects comprise most of their diet. Spawning normally takes place from late April to early June when the water reaches at least 60° F. The best artificial lures include jigs, spinners, jerkbaits, and topwater varieties.

White Bass

This cousin of the striped bass, which is native to Virginia, has a green back that blends into silver sides with a whitish belly. There are several broken horizontal lines on its sides, and the front dorsal fin is separated from the rear dorsal. Citation size in Virginia is 2½ pounds or 18 inches. White bass make an impressive spawning run in the spring from South Holston Lake up the Middle and South forks of the Holston River, and are easy to spot as they chase schools of baitfish to the surface in a feeding frenzy. The best artificial lures include jigs, bucktails, and various topwater minnow/shad imitations.

Bluegill

(Also commonly called bream.) Bluegills are members of the sunfish family. They have dark blue or green backs that fade into a silvery, yellow-green side marked by five to seven vertical bars. The cheek area is usually bluish in hue, and has a large black spot (earflap) behind the gill. While bluegills can grow to be quite large—the state record weighed 4¾ pounds—citation size in Virginia is 1 pound. These fish will eat just about anything, including crickets, worms, small minnows, and other kinds of aquatic life. They are found throughout the state's waterways and are great fighters, and the thrill of catching them likely gets young anglers hooked on fishing as adults. You will find bream in Lake Moomaw and South Holston Lake, where they spawn in late spring and early summer when the water temperature exceeds 70°F. The best artificial lures include poppers, Beetle Spins, and small soft-plastic insect imitations.

Channel Catfish

(Also referred to as a spotted cat.) Channel cats have a deeply forked tail and a spotted dark silver-gray body. Citation size in Virginia is 12 pounds or 30 inches. This species is generally a nocturnal feeder that wanders the bottom of the rivers and lakes in search of a variety of food sources, including crustaceans, fish, and carrion, and can be found throughout the waters of Virginia's Highlands, including

"Slab" crappie

the Holston River chain, South Holston Lake, and Lake Moomaw. Spotted cats spawn from late spring into early summer, and the best artificial lures include anything from jigs to crankbaits.

Flathead Catfish

(Commonly called mud cat or shovelhead cat.) True to its name, this member of the catfish family is distinguished by its flat head. The body is yellow or creamed colored with dark brown or black mottling. Citation-size fish—25 pounds or 40 inches—are found in Lake Moomaw and South Holston Lake, as well as in the South Holston River. As with most catfish, they feed at night and will eat almost anything, including other game fish. Flatheads spawn when the water temperature exceeds 72° F. Though live baits work best for flatheads, these cats have been known to hit artificial lures as well.

Crappie

(Also called speckled perch and papermouths.) There are two species of crappie—white and black. The latter is covered in black splotches and is more green on the sides, whereas the former tends to be more lightly spotted and silver-sided. Citation size is 2 pounds or 15 inches. These fish tend to congregate in submerged brush piles and fallen trees, which makes jigging for them a favorite technique of local fishermen, and their diets consist mainly of minnows and small insects. Crappie spawn in early spring when the water is around 50° F and can be caught in the shallow regions of Lake Moomaw and South Holston Lake in the springtime. The best artificial lures include jigs fished on light spinning rods, doll flies, and small crankbaits.

Muskellunge

(Also referred to as muskie.) This fish is the largest member of pike family. It is usually golden olive on the back and gray on the sides, with faint spots or blotches running vertically in a stripe-like pattern. It grows quite large, feeding on other fish, small animals, and waterfowl. Citation size in Virginia is 15 pounds or 40 inches. Muskie, which prefer clear lakes with plenty of vegetation, are stocked in the Holston River chain. The best artificial lures include big game plugs—both topwater and diving varieties—as well as large-bladed spinnerbaits.

Northern Pike

(Most often simply called pike.) These fish have long, lean bodies that are olive to green on the back and white on the belly, with horizontal rows of light colored splotches. This camouflage enables them to hide in weed beds, especially those located near drop-offs, such as river channels. Equipped with strong, tooth-lined mouths and jaws, they are voracious feeders, eating other large fish, snakes, birds, and even small mammals. Pike can get quite large; citation size in Virginia is 6 pounds or 30 inches. Reportedly stocked in Lake Moomaw in the 1990s, they are not indigenous to the commonwealth. The best artificial lures include large spoons, spinnerbaits, and big-game plugs.

Chain Pickerel

(Also called jackfish.) This member of the pike family looks very similar to the northern pike, but does not grow as large. It is distinguished by the chain-link markings on its sides and a tooth-lined mouth and jaws. Citation size in Virginia is 4 pounds or 24 inches. Pickerel are found in various rivers and reservoirs throughout the state, including Lake Moomaw, and like northern pike are most active during the cooler months of the year, when the water temperature is below 70° F. The best artificial lures include spinners, soft-plastic baits, and jerkbaits.

Redbreast Sunfish

(Also called redbelly.) This member of the sunfish family is found in the Maury and Holston rivers and is identified by the bluish stripes on its cheek and gill cover as well as a long black flap at the end of the gill plate. Redbellies feed on insects and small crustaceans and are commonly found along the banks and at the end of pools. In spring they spawn in the small gravel beds along the shoreline. Sunfish must reach 1 pound or 11 inches to be citation size in Virginia, and the best artificial lures include flies and small spinners.

Sauger

Native to the rivers and lakes of the Tennessee drainage, such as the Holston River, and smaller than its cousin the walleye, this member of the perch family is yellowish-olive, with irregular patches on its sides and a distinctive spotted dorsal fin. Sauger feed primarily near the bottom on small fish and crustaceans, and citation size in

Virginia is 2 pounds or 18 inches. The best artificial lures include spinners and jigs tipped with minnows.

Brook Trout

(Commonly known as brookie or mountain trout.) This fish species is native to the eastern mountains of the Appalachians and prolific in the many small creeks of the Virginia Highlands. Its coloring is a spectacular blend of florescent purples and yellow and red spots with faint blue rings around them. The belly is white with distinct red-orange pectoral fins that sport a vertical black-and-white stripe. Citation size in Virginia is 2 pounds or 16 inches, but a 12-inch native is considered a bragging-rights fish by state standards. These trout need clear, cold, cascading creeks with plenty of water flow and small pools. They spawn in the fall and feed mainly on aquatic insects and their larvae, as well as on various terrestrials. The best artificial lures include dry and wet flies, nymphs, and small in-line spinners.

Brown Trout

Brown trout were originally introduced from Europe. Their colors vary between olive and golden brown with red and brown spots on the sides. Large males often have a prominent hook-jaw feature and colorful orange bellies during the fall spawning period. Citation size in Virginia is 5 pounds or 25 inches. Insects, minnows, and crayfish comprise their diet. They can live in warmer and slower water than brook trout and have adapted well to the highlands, establishing a thriving wild population in such streams as Whitetop Laurel within

Blue Ridge brookie

the Mount Rogers National Recreation Area. The current state-record brown trout was caught in the South Fork of the Holston River and weighed 14 pounds, 12 ounces. The best artificial lures include dry and wet flies, streamers, spinners, and jerkbaits.

Rainbow Trout

Distinguished by its silver sides, black spots, and long pink stripe, the rainbow trout can also grow quite large—citation size in Virginia is 4 pounds or 22 inches. These fish have been imported from the Rockies and are the mainstay of the stocking program in Virginia. Wild rainbow trout can be caught in streams in the vicinity of Mount Rogers and Grayson Highlands State Park, such as Big Wilson. Both Lake Moomaw and South Holston Lake also support healthy rainbow trout populations. Their diet consists of aquatic and terrestrial insects, minnows, and various crustaceans. Rainbows spawn in the early spring months and like fast-flowing rivers as well as deep lakes. The best artificial lures include dry and wet flies, streamers, nymphs, and in-line spinners.

Walleye

Related to the sauger, and the largest member of the perch family, walleye are typically olive brown with golden-flecked sides. They grow to citation size at 5 pounds or 25 inches. These fish lie near the bottom of deeper holes in rivers by day and move onto gravel sandbars and shallow ledges to feed at night on baitfish, leeches, and crawfish. Walleye are stocked in South Holston Lake, and good spawning runs occur in the South and Middle forks of the Holston River. The best artificial lures include jigs, jerkbaits, and crankbaits.

Yellow Perch

(Also called ring perch.) Generally a yellow-green color with eight vertical grayish bars on their sides, ring perch prey on small fish and crayfish and commonly weigh 1 to 2 pounds as adults (though the state record, caught in Lake Moomaw in 1999, weighed 2 pounds, 7 ounces). They school and make spawning runs in late winter, when the water temperature reaches 45°F. While live minnows are their preferred bait, small spinners and jigs will also prove effective.

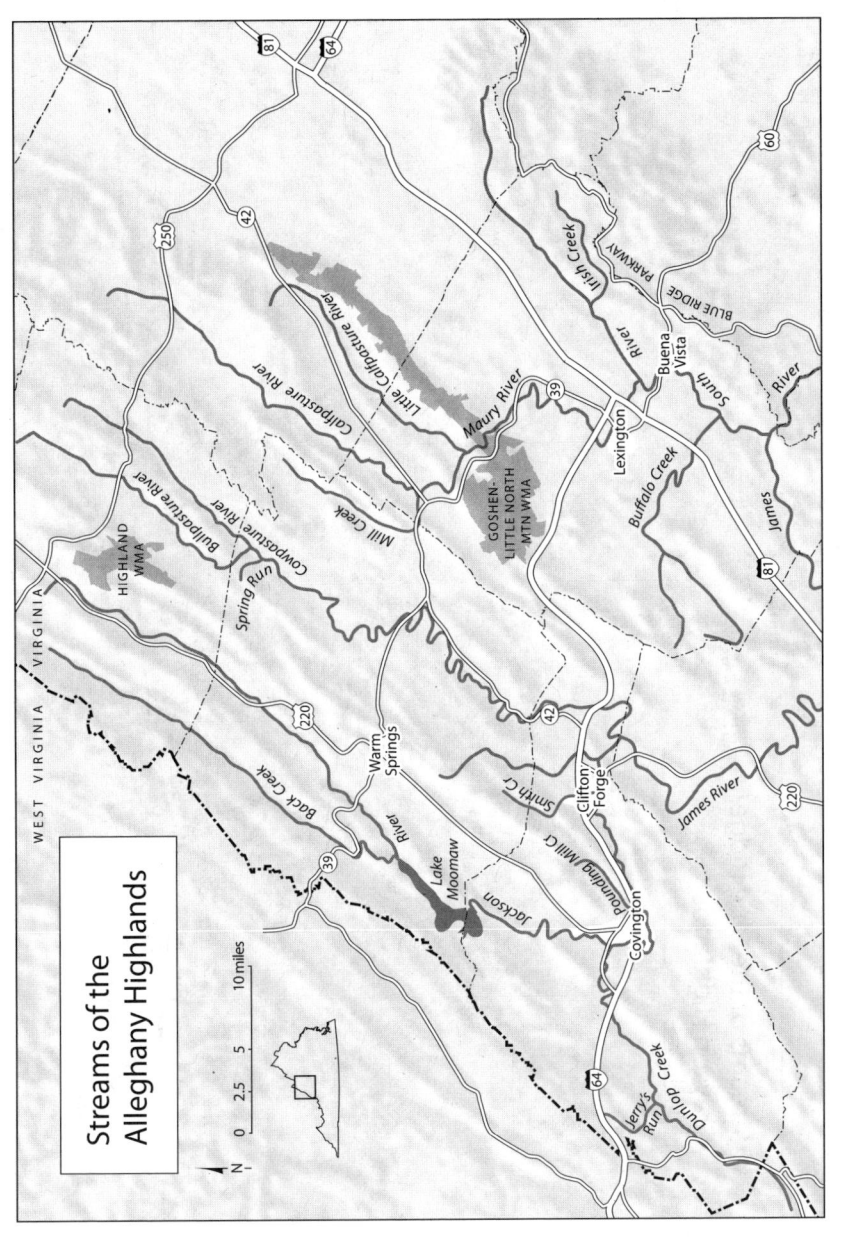

Streams of the
Alleghany Highlands

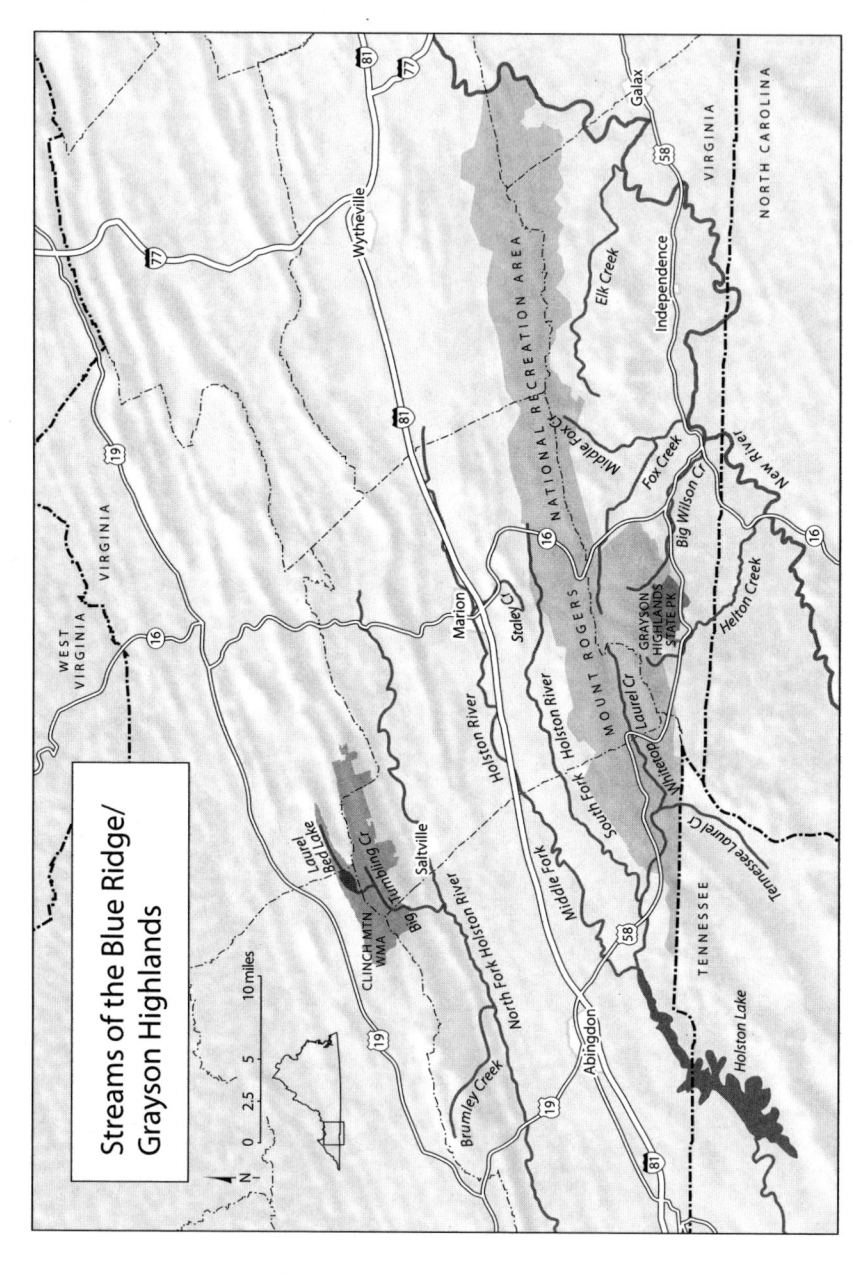

Streams of the Blue Ridge/
Grayson Highlands

Fishing for Trout

Virginia maintains a relatively healthy population of both native and stocked trout species, including brook, brown, rainbow, and golden trout. Lake Moomaw in the Alleghany Highlands regularly produces trophy brown and rainbow trout, while South Holston Lake in the Blue Ridge/Grayson Highlands has a healthy rainbow trout population. A unique feature of the highlands is that they provide both stocked and wild trout waters in close proximity. Wild trout populations (of which brook is the only native species) generally require higher elevations, with cool, well-oxygenated water (often the familiar cascading pools of the "native" creek) and a clean creek bottom on which to lay eggs. These creeks are often canopied in rhododendron and difficult to access. Due to the high elevation and dense vegetation, there are many stocked streams in the Mount Rogers National Recreation Area that support native brook trout along with wild brown and rainbow trout populations, such as the well-known and popular Whitetop Laurel (which parallels the Virginia Creeper Trail). Like many others in the area, this stream is designated special regulations and is restricted to single-hook, artificial lures only. The creel limit on streams where harvesting of trout is allowed varies, but a 7-inch minimum size limit has been imposed on all trout taken from Virginia waters.

Mount Rogers National Recreation Area and Grayson Highlands State Park

Although this is not always the case, many of the wild trout streams in these areas can be fished in a similar manner. Small in-line spinners (such as Joe's Flies) with modified single hooks can be used effectively to cast under overhangs and work the characteristically tight streams. Fly-fishermen will probably want to use shorter rods (8 feet or less) and fine tippet (6x or 7x), by way of example. I have found dry-fly patterns such as Royal Wulffs and Blue Wing Olives to be most effective. Prince and Hare's Ear nymphs are good choices in the colder months and the deeper runs. Above all, fish upstream whenever possible (employing roll casts to counter the underbrush and overhanging trees) and practice stealth to catch these wild beauties! Since camping is allowed within the National Forest boundaries, backpacking in from the numerous trails is a great way to fish the more remote sections of many of these creeks. By applying and adapting these techniques to individual streams, you should have success catching wild trout in this extraordinary area.

Nearly 15 miles of wild trout streams lie within the Grayson Highlands State Park itself, located off U.S. 58 in Grayson County (see the appendix, p. 76, for directions and other information). Unfortunately, like so much of the habitat of the Southern Appalachian brook trout, this watershed is threatened by acid rain, which highlights the delicate nature of this fragile fishery. Special regulations apply to all of these streams, including Big Wilson, Little Wilson, Wilburn Branch, Mill Creek, Quebec Branch, and Cabin Creek. All trout less than 9 inches must be released and state creel limits apply. A permit is also required when fishing on National Forest property.

Big Wilson Creek runs along the northeastern boundary of the park and offers over 3 miles of fishable water. From its headwaters to a sign below its confluence with Little Wilson Creek, the stream is designated special regulations. You can reach the creek via the Appalachian Trail at Massie Gap or by taking the Big Wilson Creek Trail from the main campground in the park.

Little Wilson Creek is also designated special regulations for all portions within Grayson Highlands State Park.

Wilburn Branch is located in the center of the park and provides 2 miles of designated special-regulation wild trout water. It can be accessed via the Stamper's Branch or Upchurch Road trail.

Mill Creek offers a mile of fishable water in the park's southeastern corner. It too is designated a special-regulation wild trout stream. Turn left at the park's entrance on VA 742 (Mill Creek Road) to access it.

Quebec Branch is located in the park's northern region, with a mile of fishable water that is designated special regulations. You can access it from the Appalachian Trail at Massie Gap or by taking

Fly-fishing in the Grayson Highlands

Wilson Creek Trail at the main campground to the Seed Orchard Road Trail.

Cabin Creek is found on the park's western side and has 2 miles of fishable water that hold only wild rainbow and native brook trout. Anglers must take Cabin Creek Trail at Massie Gap to reach it.

Stocked Highland Waters by County

There are approximately 600 miles of stocked fishable trout water in Virginia, and over one million fish are stocked annually (from October to June), according to Virginia Department of Game and Inland Fisheries (VDGIF). A Virginia trout fishing license is required on these waters, together with a National Forest stamp when fishing within its boundaries. *Note:* From June 16 through the month of September anglers can fish in stocked waters without a trout license. The streams discussed in the following pages are traditionally stocked by the VDGIF. Bear in mind that the list is not exhaustive; you can check the latest stream stockings by county before you plan a trip by phoning (434) 525-FISH (3474). Stocking schedules and other information can also be obtained online at www.dgif.virginia. gov. Note that here and elsewhere in the book, each watercourse name is accompanied by a reference to the page on which it can be found in DeLorme's *Virginia Atlas and Gazetteer* (6th edition; see the appendix, p. 81).

These are the stocking categories according to the VDGIF trout-stocking schedule; note that they are subject to change:

CATEGORY A: Stocked once in October, November/December, January/February; twice in March, April; and once in May.

CATEGORY B: Stocked once in November/December, January/February, March; and twice April 1 through May 15.

CATEGORY C: Stocked three times between October and April.

NSF: Waters do not receive fall and early winter stockings.

SPECIAL REGULATION: Single-hook, artificial lures only; no bait may be in angler's possession, and varying minimum size limits apply.

DH: Delayed Harvest waters; catch-and-release and artificial lures only from October 1 through May 31.

The rest of this chapter covers the majority of the stocked streams in Virginia's Highlands and provides the location of and directions to each. In addition to these streams, some of the smaller stocked lakes in these regions include Laurel Bed Lake (no permit required; see pp. 40–41) and Lexington City Reservoir (permit required from Lexington City Hall, [540] 462-3702).

Alleghany Highlands

Alleghany County

Jackson River—Tailwater (Formerly stocked below Lake Moomaw and Gathright Dam)

VIRGINIA ATLAS AND GAZETTEER: 52

DIRECTIONS: From I-64 at Covington, take U.S. 220 north until you see the signs for Lake Moomaw, and turn left at the signs onto VA 687. Proceed approximately 3 miles, then turn left onto VA 666 and follow this to VA 605, which will take you to the dam. You'll find parking and access to the tailwater below the dam via a feeder road off VA 605.

This was supposed to be one of the premier tailwater trout fisheries on the East Coast when stocking was originally proposed, but disputes about water rights between property owners and fishermen has quelled that enthusiasm. Below Gathright Dam, six public areas (spaced roughly 3 miles apart) provide access to almost 19 miles of navigable water to Covington. These are found immediately below Gathright Dam, as well as at Johnson Spring, Smith Bridge, Indian

Wild brown trout

Draft, Petticoat Junction, and just upstream of the Westvaco Dam in Covington. Wade fishing can be quite productive around these areas, but because some private landowners have established exclusive private rights, float-fishing is not advised. While wild rainbow and brown trout can be caught (12-inch minimum size limit, 4 fish per day creel limit), no "special regulations" are in place. Rainbows up to 20 inches in length and even larger brown trout are not uncommon.

I float-fished this water in the mid-1990s when it was still stocked and enjoyed both the beauty of this splendid river and the bounty that a truly well-managed trout habitat can yield. Hopefully, this opportunity will again be available one day soon to Virginia's anglers. The Verona office of the Virginia Department of Game and Inland Fisheries (see the appendix, p. 77) is a good source of information; for specifics concerning water levels and power generation at the Gathright Dam contact the U.S. Army Corps of Engineers, Covington, Virginia, (540) 962-1138.

Jerry's Run (Category A; located within the George Washington National Forest)

VIRGINIA ATLAS AND GAZETTEER: 52

DIRECTIONS: From I-64 at Covington, take U.S. 60 west to FR 69 at Lewis Mountain and turn left. Jerry's Run is situated between Lewis and Brushy mountains along the Alleghany County border with West Virginia and is stocked along FR 69.

Pounding Mill Creek (Category A; located within the George Washington National Forest)

VIRGINIA ATLAS AND GAZETTEER: 52

DIRECTIONS: From I-64 at Covington, take U.S. 220 north, then take VA 625 north until it reaches the creek and turn onto FR 125, which runs parallel to the water. This relatively small stream has both wild brook and rainbow trout and is also stocked for put-and-take fishing. Fly-fisherman will need short rods (6 to 7 feet) with 2– to 3–weight line. For flies, try size 18 Royal Wulffs and caddis imitations. Spin fisherman should use small, in-line spinners such as Joe's Flies for success with both stocked and wild trout.

Smith Creek (NSF, Special Regulations [single-hook, artificial lures only, 12–inch minimum size limit]; located within the George Washington National Forest)

VIRGINIA ATLAS AND GAZETTEER: 52

DIRECTIONS: From I-64 at Clifton Forge, take VA 606 north to the creek. To reach the more remote upper section where wild brook trout fishing is possible, bear right onto FR 125.

The special regulations section of Smith Creek extends from the Clifton Forge Dam downstream 2.5 miles to the Forest Service boundary above the old C&O Dam. Fingerling brown trout are stocked annually, with fish reaching up to 20 inches. This stream provides good fly-fishing, with wide, flat pools. Access is via VA 606 from Clifton Forge to the Clifton Forge Water plant, where fishermen must park and walk half a mile to the creek.

BIG FISH TIP *There is also a put-and-take section above the dam and wild brookie fishing farther upstream of that. Parachute Adams will produce strikes on this section.*

Bath County

Back Creek (Category A, Delayed Harvest (DH); located within the George Washington National Forest)

VIRGINIA ATLAS AND GAZETTEER: 64

DIRECTIONS: Take VA 39 west from Warm Springs about 10 miles until you see the stocking signs on the left to reach the put-and-take water; continue about 4 miles, then turn right on VA 600 and follow this road for 6 miles to reach the delayed harvest section. Delayed harvest restrictions apply to that portion of the stream from the VA 600 bridge (below Back Creek Dam and Reservoir) downstream 1.5 miles to the VA 600 bridge at the lower boundary of the Bath County Recreation Area.

If you like to fish big streams that flow through rugged mountainous terrain, yet offer relatively easy access, Back Creek is for you! There are over 3 miles of put-and-take water along VA 39 near Warm Springs, above the confluence with the Jackson River. You can camp at Blowing Spring Recreation Area in the national forest. The water here is big—up to 75 feet wide during spring flow. The delayed harvest water averages about 25 feet wide and is located below the weirs at the Bath County Recreation Area. There is a gravel pull-off on the right just before the VA 600 bridge for parking, and a trail that leads up the stream.

At the footbridge over the creek you'll find a large, languid pool of water where my wife and I were able to hook several nice trout in early March of 2005. There is a large boulder near the bottom of the pool that creates a nice riffle where we caught two nice browns on GCO Buggers that day. Just above the bridge, the right bank features subsurface boulders, where we landed four nice rainbows on March Brown droppers. Farther downstream, I pulled a tiny native brook trout from a rapid. As our experience attests, this stream has a little of everything to offer a savvy angler.

Bullpasture River (Category A; stocked above Williamsville in the Highland State Wildlife Management Area)

VIRGINIA ATLAS AND GAZETTEER: 65

DIRECTIONS: From Warm Springs, take VA 39 east to VA 629 and turn left; then turn left again onto VA 625 north. After about 5 miles, this road will turn into VA 678; follow this to Williamsville and the Highland State Wildlife Management Area, where the river is stocked.

This splendid put-and-take stream is stocked in the southern corner of the Highland State Wildlife Management Area, which extends into Bath County just above the confluence with the Cowpasture at Williamsville along VA 678, and along VA 628 below the VA 614 bridge. The upper section flows through a spectacular gorge area that is difficult to access, but well worth the effort. You will need a long rod here to cast far distances in the huge pools formed by the mammoth boulders.

> **BIG FISH TIP** *Although it isn't officially stocked, there is good trout and small-mouth fishing in the Cowpasture River below where Spring Run (Category A) enters the river. Note: Much of the Cowpasture River lies in private property and will require landowner permission to fish; however, there is an access trail at a primitive camping area within the George Washington National Forest on VA 678, just below the Coursey Springs Fish Hatchery.*

Jackson River (Category A, Special Regulations; located above Lake Moomaw in Hidden Valley, within the George Washington National Forest)

VIRGINIA ATLAS AND GAZETTEER: 64/65

DIRECTIONS: Take VA 39 west from Warm Springs about 4 miles until you see the signs indicating "Recreation Area." Turn right onto VA 621 at the sign, then left again at the next sign. The Hidden Valley Campground entrance is on the left, and you will find stocking signs and a parking area a quarter mile farther down the road. There is another access upstream, at Poor Farm, along VA 623 (off U.S. 220).

The trout fishing is outstanding year round in the spectacular upper reaches of this stream above Lake Moomaw, within the George

Jackson River release

Washington National Forest. Large, lake-run rainbow trout can be caught here during the early spring, and stocked fish can also be found. The stream is stocked at Poor Farm, along VA 623 (off U.S. 220), and above Hidden Valley Campground on VA 621 (off VA 39). There is a 3-mile stretch of special regulation water (16-inch minimum, 2-trout limit) above the Muddy Run swinging bridge and below the Poor Farm area (off VA 623). You will have to hike into this area along a footpath (Forest Service Road 481) from either of the access points noted above. There are also primitive camping areas along this portion of the stream. CAUTION: During the spring months, heavy rains and snowmelts can combine to strand camping fisherman here.

This is a fairly large stream, averaging 50 feet across during full flow, with pockets, runs, deep holes, and pools. It is stocked with rainbow, brown, and brook trout. Small in-line spinners work great on the put-and-take sections, and large buggers, Pheasant Tails, Brown Caddis, and March Browns have all produced fish on this lovely water, including a fine 12-inch brook trout that my wife caught on one outing we fondly recall. The only way to do this stream justice is to camp along the bank and spend a few days getting to know it; you will be well rewarded.

BIG FISH TIP   *Try Muddy Run, a feeder stream that enters at the bottom of the special regulation section, for wild trout fishing.*

Spring Run (Category A, Special Regulations: catch-and-release only from June 16 through September 30; regular put-and-take rules apply during the rest of the year)

VIRGINIA ATLAS AND GAZETTEER: 65

DIRECTIONS: From Warm Springs, take VA 39 east to VA 629 and turn left, then turn left again onto VA 625 north. After about 5 miles, this road will turn into VA 678; proceed until you see a sign for the stream on your right.

This beautiful spring-fed stream flows out of the Coursey Springs State Fish Hatchery. Needless to say, it stays well stocked! I prefer to fish the lower section beyond view of the hatchery. There is a path that leads downstream towards the Cowpasture River.

BIG FISH TIP *When all the other creeks in the area are running high and muddy, this baby will be clear and full of fish!*

Rockbridge County

Buffalo Creek (Designated Trophy Trout Stream, Special Regulations)

VIRGINIA ATLAS AND GAZETTEER: 53

DIRECTIONS: Buffalo Creek can be reached by taking VA 251 south from Lexington. From I-81, take the VA 60 exit toward Lexington, then follow signs to VA 251 south, which leads you to the lower boundary of the stream; turn left onto VA 612 (Bluegrass Trail) to reach the top of the special regulations section.

The upper boundary of Buffalo Creek Fishing Area begins at the parking area (denoted by a wooden "special regulations" sign) below the confluence of the North and South forks of Buffalo Creek and extends downstream 3 miles to the confluence of Colliers Creek (at the intersection of VA 612 and VA 251). *Note:* There is a "fish sanctuary" near the lower boundary limit where fishing is prohibited, designated by a sign hanging on a cable that crosses the river. A second parking and access area lies upstream of the sanctuary at the intersection of VA 612 and VA 677. To fish the stream you'll need a permit, which is available by writing the Virginia Department of Game and Inland Fisheries office in Verona (see the appendix, p. 77, for their address, and include a self-addressed stamped envelope). Brown and rainbow fingerlings are stocked annually by the VDGIF, and a 16-inch, 2 fish per day limit applies to the stream.

This medium-gradient, freestone creek averages about 25 feet wide and offers a variety of fishing conditions, including slow, deep pools following long runs, undercut banks, and bends with overhanging trees. Caddis, mayfly, and midge hatches provide regular meals for the brown and rainbow trout, as does an abundance of large minnows and crayfish. Try attractor patterns, such as Adams Parachutes, in the spring; various terrestrials, such as beetles, are good summer bets.

The headwaters of Buffalo Creek flow out of the highlands to the west into a scenic valley where the stream is stocked. I fished the stream one Christmas Eve when the peaks were covered with snow and the valley was experiencing the end of a recent melt. The water was up and flowing well, creating ideal conditions for "nymphing" after wild trout, which you'll also find in Buffalo.

BIG FISH TIP *Try North Buffalo Creek for plunge-pool-style wild trout fishing.*

Irish Creek (Category B; located within the George Washington National Forest, off Blue Ridge Parkway, near Buena Vista)
VIRGINIA ATLAS AND GAZETTEER: 54
DIRECTIONS: Irish Creek is stocked on Irish Creek Road, north of Buena Vista. To reach the stream, take South River Road north from U.S. 60 in Buena Vista for about 5 miles until you pass the town of Cornwall, then turn right onto Irish Creek Road. Stocking signs are visible along the creek, which parallels the road. This typical parkway stream may yield an occasional native trout to the stealthy fisherman.

Maury River (Category A; Goshen–Little North Mountain Wildlife Management Area at Goshen Pass)
VIRGINIA ATLAS AND GAZETTEER: 53
DIRECTIONS: From I-64 at Lexington, take exit 55 onto U.S. 11 north to reach VA 39 west, then travel 12 miles into Goshen Pass and Little North Mountain Wildlife Management Area, where the stream is stocked. Numerous pull-offs along VA 39 allow wade access to the river.

The Maury River through Goshen Pass is simply spectacular. The pass is about 4 miles long and full of rocks, falls, ledges, and rapids. Stocking begins at the Goshen Pass Wayside (which is equipped with bathrooms and picnic tables) and extends upstream to the swinging bridge, where you'll find hiking trails and primitive camping facilities. You can reach the other side of the river, away from the road, by crossing the bridge and following the footpath that extends downstream for a half a mile, allowing wade fishermen to work otherwise inaccessible water. I like to take this route to fish for holdover rainbow trout on the Maury, which are plentiful throughout the pass. Besides trout, you may also catch smallmouth bass and redeye (rock bass) in this portion of the river.

This is big water by Virginia standards, over 100 feet wide in places, especially during the spring trout season when water levels often peak. Light spinning rods and 9-foot, 5- to 6-weight fly-rods are best for making the long casts needed to cover this stream. Try small crankbaits and in-line spinners for trout and bass on spinning rods, and Woolly Buggers and dry flies on the long rod. CAUTION: I recommend wearing a PFD (personal floatation device) while wading the Maury, especially when stream flow is high.

BIG FISH TIP *For a shot at some wild rainbows, try Laurel Run near the wayside; take the hunter's access trailhead at VA 39.*

Mill Creek (Category A; located within the George Washington National Forest)
VIRGINIA ATLAS AND GAZETTEER: 53
DIRECTIONS: From I-64 at Lexington, take exit 55 onto U.S. 11 north,

then turn left onto VA 39 west and go past the Goshen–Little North Mountain Wildlife Management Area and turn left onto VA 42, where the stream is stocked.

South River (Category B)

VIRGINIA ATLAS AND GAZETTEER: 54

DIRECTIONS: The South River is stocked along South River Road northeast of Buena Vista, which you can reach from U.S. 60. Travel north until you see stocking signs along the road where it parallels the stream between the towns of Vesuvius and Buena Vista.

Blue Ridge/Grayson Highlands

Grayson County

Big Wilson (Category A, Special Regulations; located within Grayson Highlands State Park/Mount Rogers National Recreation Area)

VIRGINIA ATLAS AND GAZETTEER: 23

DIRECTIONS: Access can be gained through trails in Grayson Highlands State Park (VA 362/VA 806) or from the bottom via VA 817 off U.S. 58, west of the city of Galax. From the I-77 exit at Hillsville, take U.S. 58 west through Galax into Grayson Highlands State Park. Turn right onto VA 817 at the creek, then take the next left onto Peace Haven Road and follow until it ends.

You'll find native brook and wild rainbow trout in this stream's headwaters and its tributaries, but be aware that special regulations (single-hook, artificial lures only, 9-inch minimum size) apply throughout Grayson Highlands State Park. Big Wilson has spectacular scenery—large boulders, waterfalls, and deep pristine pools. A rough trail parallels the stream, but allows for adequate access in rugged terrain.

This is great water for wild trout enthusiasts and put-and-take fisherman alike. The lower portion of the stream is stocked for 3 to 4 miles running along U.S. 58. The upper portion, within the Grayson Highlands State Park, is subject to special regulations. I have had my best luck here on dry flies during late winter and early spring; fish upstream with caddis imitations and Royal Wulff patterns in sizes 18 to 20 during this time of year for the best action. The wild rainbows here are gorgeous specimens with a golden hue and distinct red stripes and gill plates.

BIG FISH TIP *Try the Little Wilson prong, on which special regulations apply.*

Elk Creek (Category A)

VIRGINIA ATLAS AND GAZETTEER: 23

DIRECTIONS: From the I-77 exit at Hillsville, take U.S. 58 west through Galax to VA 21 at Independence and turn right. To reach the upper, stocked portions of Elk Creek, go 9 miles to VA 658 and turn left. Follow this road for about 2 miles to VA 663 and turn left. The stream is stocked near the town of Elk Creek at various points between Powder Mill Road bridge (VA 663) and Falls Road bridge (VA 662). Here, Elk Creek is low gradient with medium width, averaging about 15 feet across. The lower reaches of the stream are also stocked along VA 660 and 650 near Carsonville (Clito), and are prime trout water by southwest Virginia standards. To reach this section, follow the directions above, but turn right off VA 21 onto VA 660 before you reach VA 658.

BIG FISH TIP *There is a spectacular 40-foot waterfall visible from Falls Road (VA 662) about a mile past the intersection with VA 611, which is well worth checking out if you are in the region.*

Fox Creek and Middle Fox Creek (Category B; located within the Jefferson National Forest)

VIRGINIA ATLAS AND GAZETTEER: 23

DIRECTIONS: To reach Fox Creek, from the I-77 exit at Hillsville, take U.S. 58 west through Independence to VA 16 north. Travel on VA 16 north about 10 miles and turn left onto VA 603 at Troutdale. Fox Creek is stocked along VA 603 within the National Forest boundaries to the Fairwood Cemetery bridge, where parking is available. To reach Middle Fox Creek, from U.S. 58 take a right onto VA 711 (Fox Creek Road) at Fox and travel about 2 miles until you reach VA 678. Middle Fox is stocked upstream along VA 678 to the intersection with VA 658.

Fox Creek is a high-gradient, tight, laurel-lined creek. Fly-fishing can be quite difficult, and a short rod is a plus. Spin fishing is probably most effective here. Middle Fox is much larger than its sister creek and is suited to both spin and fly-fishing. It is easily accessible for about 2 miles via VA 678. Since both streams are designated put-

and-take waters that run along roadsides, don't expect to find many holdover fish.

Helton Creek (Category B)

VIRGINIA ATLAS AND GAZETTEER: 22

DIRECTIONS: From I-77 at Hillsville, take U.S. 58 west through Galax into Grayson Highlands State Park, then turn right onto VA 783, which parallels the stream. There is a parking area and a foot trail at the end of VA 783 where it enters the Jefferson National Forest, which allows access to the upper reaches of the creek.

Helton Creek is stocked along U.S. 58 below VA 783. This mid-size stream (up to 20 feet wide in places) offers good put-and-take fishing in this area. Farther upstream, you'll find that plunge pools, waterfalls, and short runs characterize this stretch of classic native trout water. Downstream, near its confluence with the New River (in our sister state of North Carolina), Helton is a formidable creek with delayed-harvest designation.

Smyth County

Middle Fork of the Holston (Category A, Heritage Day program; located near Marion)

VIRGINIA ATLAS AND GAZETTEER: 23

DIRECTIONS: Take I-81 to exit 16 at Marion. A mile section of the stream is stocked in downtown Marion between Broad Street and the town park. River Walk Trail, which runs from the park alongside the river, allows easy access to this area. The Middle Fork is a designated Heritage Day stream, a throwback to when the "opening day" of trout season (always the first Saturday in April) drew lines of fisherman to the banks of their favorite waters to swap fish tales and fishing holes.

While the VDGIF's new stocking procedures have pretty much done away with this "elbow to elbow" opening-day scenario, anglers who enjoyed the camaraderie and competition can still experience it by fishing Heritage Day waters like the Middle Fork on the first Saturday in April every year. Bring a kid and introduce him or her to fishing—there are always plenty of fish to catch on Heritage Day here!

BIG FISH TIP *If you want to avoid the downtown traffic, there is another section (Dry Fork) on the upper end of the river that is stocked off of U.S. 11 at Groseclose.*

South Fork of the Holston (Category A, Special Regulations; located at Buller Fish Hatchery within Mount Rogers National Recreation Area and Jefferson National Forest)

VIRGINIA ATLAS AND GAZETTEER: 23

DIRECTIONS: The South Fork of the Holston can be reached via VA 16, west of Sugar Grove near the Appalachian Trail crossing. From I-81 in Marion, take the VA 16 exit to Mount Rogers National Recreation Area. Go south until you reach Sugar Grove, then turn right onto VA 601 (Teas Road). The river is soon visible, and after about 3 miles you will reach the special regulations area.

South Fork, Holston River

This 4-mile stretch (single-hook, artificial lures only, with a 16-inch minimum, 2-trout limit) runs from a sign at the Jefferson National Forest boundary downstream to 500 feet above the concrete dam at Buller Fish Hatchery. The very rugged gorgelike terrain holds excellent populations of both wild rainbow and brown trout, and there are numerous roadside pull-offs that allow stream access. You'll find a catch-and-release-only section from the dam downstream to the lower limit of the hatchery property. There is put-and-take fishing in the pond just above the dam at the hatchery, and a separate put-and-take area near Chilhowie. You can reach the Buller Fish Hatchery property from VA 650 south of Marion, or by following the directions above and continuing past the special regulations area on VA 601 until you reach South Holston River Road (VA 650).

I prefer fishing the South Fork of the Holston in the winter months when the pressure is light and the angling is often superb. Pheasant Tail and Hare's Ear nymphs are usually "go-to" flies that time of year, but there are also winter Blue Wing Olive hatches on this stream that can make for terrific dry-fly opportunities. I have witnessed surface feeding frenzies on microscopic blue wings in subfreezing temperatures along the catch-and-release-only section of the South Fork at Buller Fish Hatchery. These astonishing events often last for only five or ten minutes in mid-afternoon, frequently ending as abruptly as they began.

My favorite area to fish is the special regulation section above the hatchery where the Appalachian Trail crosses the river; there is a pretty good stretch of water upstream of here to the National Forest boundary. I have seen fish nearly 24 inches long in these waters. Another good run begins at the first bridge you come to downstream of the trail crossing. (Avoid the quarter mile or so immediately upstream of the bridge.) Here the stream winds well away from the road and offers some spectacular fishing.

BIG FISH TIP *Three tributaries of the South Fork—Cressy Creek, Comers Creek, and Dickey Creek—receive Category C stockings.*

Staley Creek (Category A)

VIRGINIA ATLAS AND GAZETTEER: 23

DIRECTIONS: From I-81 in Marion, turn south onto VA 16; Staley

Creek is stocked this stretch of road, downstream of the state fish hatchery. Due to its location, this little put-and-take stream sees a lot of fishing pressure.

Washington County

Big Tumbling Creek (Category A; Clinch Mountain Fee Fishing Area)

VIRGINIA ATLAS AND GAZETTEER: 22

DIRECTIONS: From I-81 at Chilhowie, take the Saltville exit north onto VA 107. When you reach VA 91 (Main Street) in Saltville, turn left, then take a right onto Allison Gap Road (VA 634) and go north from town to Poor Valley Road (VA 613) and turn left again. Go west until you reach VA 747 and turn right. This road parallels the creek and leads to the fee fishing area within the 25,000-acre Clinch Mountain Wildlife Management Area. The stream is designated put-and-take fishing until you reach the bridge at the WMA entrance. (There are signs that indicate you have entered the fee fishing area.) A Virginia Department of Game and Inland Fisheries headquarters is located a bit farther up the road on the right; however, you must purchase permits in advance via the VDGIF's new electronic sales system. Go to www.dfig.virginia.gov to locate a license agent or to purchase permits and licenses online, or phone (866) 693-9157 toll free. During the winter months when inclement weather may force closing of the area, you may also want to contact the VDGIF's Marion office at (276) 783-4860 or the Clinch Mountain Wildlife Management Area office at (276) 944-3434 prior to your trip.

Stocked rainbow trout

Located in the upper corner of Washington and Smyth counties, Big Tumbling is a gorgeous stream that gets its name from the many pools, waterfalls, and runs that form as it "tumbles" down from the spur atop the Clinch Mountain Range. In all, there are close to 5 miles of fishable water in the entire wildlife management area, which extends into Russell County. The stream is stocked daily (except on Sundays) from the first Saturday in April through September 30, and thus is a favorite of local put-and-take fisherman once the regular state stocking season ends in June. I have fished the stream at that time of year and can attest to its popularity. Fishing is allowed from 6 AM until 8 PM daily. Standard creel limits (6 fish per day, 7-inch minimum size) apply to all fish kept, and there are both stocked rainbow and wild brook trout to be found here. Most anglers use spinning rods with night crawlers or power bait, and head home with a full stringer of fish for the frying pan.

BIG FISH TIP *Laurel Bed Creek and Laurel Bed Lake in Russell County are also stocked and are well worth the trip to the top of the Clinch Mountain Wildlife Management Area (for more information see p. 75.)*

Brumley Creek (Category C; north of Abingdon)

VIRGINIA ATLAS AND GAZETTEER: 21

DIRECTIONS: From I-81, take the Abingdon exit, then follow U.S. 19 north to VA 211. Turn right and go about 3 miles until you reach VA 687 and turn left. The creek is stocked along VA 687.

BIG FISH TIP *Try Big Brumley Creek at nearby Hidden Valley Lake for fantastic trout fishing in a remote setting.*

Laurel Bed Lake (located within the Clinch Mountain Wildlife Management Area)

VIRGINIA ATLAS AND GAZETTEER: 22

DIRECTIONS: From I-81 at Chilhowie, take the Saltville exit north onto VA 107. When you reach VA 91 (Main Street) in Saltville, turn left, then take a right onto Allison Gap Road (VA 634) and go north from town to Poor Valley Road (VA 613) and turn left again. Go west until you reach VA 747 and turn right. This lengthy road parallels Big Tumbling Creek and leads to the lake, which rests atop Clinch Mountain at 3,600 feet in elevation.

This 330-acre lake offers the kind of spectacular beauty reminiscent of Sierra lakes on the West Coast and is currently managed for brook trout, smallmouth bass, and rock bass. Routine fisheries management activities include fish population sampling and water quality improvement (through liming). A sustainable brook trout population is augmented by a regular stocking program in the fall, which provides fishing opportunities throughout the year. Fishing usually becomes more difficult during the summer months as the lake temperature increases. My favorite summer fishing spots are located around well-shaded coves where spring branches enter. While summer and early fall trout fishing can be sporadic, both are excellent times to catch trophy smallmouth bass, which must be returned unharmed as the developing fishery is catch-and-release-only. Camping is permitted within the management area and a concession stand is in operation during the summer. No fee is required.

Tennessee Laurel (Category A; near Damascus)

VIRGINIA ATLAS AND GAZETTEER: 22

DIRECTIONS: From I-81 north of Abingdon, take U.S. 58 south to Damascus, then follow VA 91 south, where the stream is stocked. This smaller tributary of Whitetop Laurel receives fewer accolades than its nearby cousin, but offers locals some fine put-and-take fishing.

Whitetop Laurel (Category A, Special Regulations; located in Mount Rogers National Recreation Area, within the Jefferson National Forest)

VIRGINIA ATLAS AND GAZETTEER: 22

DIRECTIONS: From I-81 north of Abingdon, take U.S. 58 south past Damascus where the stream is stocked. Access, parking, and bathroom facilities are located at the Straight Branch and Creek Junction entry points indicated by the Virginia Creeper Trail signs along U.S. 58.

Whitetop Laurel has both put-and-take and two special regulation sections, the first of which runs about 4 miles from the mouth of Green Cove Creek downstream to the first railroad bridge above Taylors Valley. Access to this section is via VA 728, off of U.S. 58. The second special regulations section extends downstream from a sign at the Forest Service boundary just below the put-and-take portion of Taylors Valley (access via VA 725, off VA 91) to the mouth of Straight Branch, which is also stocked along U.S. 58 (access off of U.S. 58). Single-hook, artificial lures only, and a 12-inch minimum size limit apply to these areas. *Note:* The first special regulations section extends upstream a mile into Green Cove Creek, off VA 859.

This beautiful mountain stream, along which the Virginia Creeper Trail runs, gets its name from the heavy laurel and rhododendron plants that protect the fishery. High-gradient runs, boulders, log-jam-choked pools, and cold, gin-clear water characterize the creek, creating a veritable trout paradise in which both wild rainbow and brown trout can be caught, along with stocked fish of the same species. Some of the best fly-fishing on Whitetop Laurel occurs from late spring into early June, when sulphur mayflies are plentiful and an exceptional green drake hatch takes place. Size 18 Blue Quills are a good bet during the winter months. Spin fishermen may opt to use single-hook Joe's Flies in the special regulation sections.

BIG FISH TIP *An excellent way to access the 12 miles of water between Creek Junction and Damascus Caboose is by cycling the trail; shuttles are available at a number of the bicycle liveries in Damascus, such as Blue Blaze Bike and Shuttle Service (see the appendix, p. 78).*

3

Fishing Lake Moomaw and the Maury River

Interestingly, these two popular bodies of water in the Alleghany Highlands originate as tributaries of the James River. Lake Moomaw, located within the George Washington National Forest in Bath County, is an impoundment of the Jackson River that eventually joins the Cowpasture River at Iron Gate to form the James River. Beginning near Goshen Pass, where the Calfpasture River meets the Little Calfpasture, the Maury flows its entire length through Rockbridge County until it reaches the James River at Glasgow. Both offer their visitors wonderful fishing and other recreational activities.

Lake Moomaw

VIRGINIA ATLAS AND GAZETTEER: 52

Directions: From I-64 at Covington, take U.S. 220 north until you see the signs for Lake Moomaw, then turn left onto VA 687. After approximately 3 miles, turn left onto VA 666, and follow this road to reach the Fortney Branch landing at the bottom of the lake. To access the Coles Point launch, just before reaching the landing, turn right onto VA 605, which will take you across the dam.

Lake Moomaw is a splendid highland lake in every sense of the term. This scenic, 2,530-acre reservoir, 12 miles long and very deep (averaging nearly 100 feet), is located almost entirely within the Gathright Wildlife Management Area, which is operated by the Virginia Department of Game and Inland Fisheries. There are numerous camping and recreational areas (some primitive) around the lake. You can camp, swim, and picnic at the Bolar Mountain Recreation Area, where you'll also find restrooms. For maps and facility information, contact the George Washington and Jefferson National Forests in Covington at (540) 962-2214, and in Hot Springs at (540) 839-2521.

Fishing off the shoreline can be very rewarding here, as the lake is nearly totally surrounded by public property. John Kemp, who is a Lake Moomaw fanatic, told me about a shoreline excursion he made one spring, where he witnessed thousands of rainbows schooled up in the Fortney Branch arm of the lake, and caught numerous fish from the bank on spinners. Although the lake is generally deep, there are shallow flats, humps, tree stumps, and man-made structures that can be accessed via the shore. While these provide great habitat for the plethora of game fish here, they also create underwater hazards for boaters, who should be especially careful to avoid subsurface structures between the months of November and February when the lake is typically drawn down.

A variety of great angling opportunities exist year round on Lake

Moomaw. Both largemouth and smallmouth bass are found here, with smallmouth predominating. Smallies in excess of 4 pounds are not uncommon, but remember that there is a 12-inch size limit on all bass creeled on the lake. Jerkbaits, lipless crankbaits such as Rattle Traps, and plastic jigs and worms—particularly blue- and black-colored ones—will all work well. In the early spring, try casting crankbaits from McClintic Bridge downstream for both species of black bass. Lake Moomaw is Virginia's top producer of yellow perch—the state record was caught here in 1999—and crappie fishing is quite good as well. Fall and spring months are best for locat-

Lake Moomaw

ing schools of both species by jigging around subsurface structures, trolling small deep-diving minnow plugs like Rapala Countdowns, or casting Silver Buddies. Spring trout fishing at the lake can also be productive, especially around points and creek mouths. A trout license is not required; however, a 16-inch size minimum and 2-fish limit is in effect. Large brown and rainbow trout (which sometimes reach over 10 pounds) can be caught by using live alewives or trolling imitation shad lures (such as Redfin plugs or Johnson spoons) at various depths, normally at 15 to 25 feet with the boat sitting in 40 to 50 feet of water. Chain pickerel are also found in the lake; fish for them with large plugs on flats and near drop-offs in shallow bays.

As you might have sensed, the question here is not whether you'll catch fish, but what kind you'll land. The answer usually depends on the time of year that you visit. Warm water species such as black bass, catfish, and panfish are abundant during the summer months, while cold water species such as trout and yellow perch are more likely to be caught in the winter. The most exciting time to be on the lake, though, is in the fall and spring, when "turnover" occurs. During this period, you may catch any or all of these fish on a single outing! Normally in the winter or summer the water temperature in large lakes and reservoirs stratifies, with the topmost layers close to air temperature, and the deeper layers warmer in winter and cooler in summer. During turnover, as the warmer and cooler water trade places, the layers mix and create a thermocline where fish congregate. Under these conditions you can cast Crocodile spoons from midlake regions toward the shore and work them back to the boat at different depths by varying the retrieval speed until you locate fish. This tactic will also work from the shoreline. John Kemp and I enjoyed some great fall fishing one November when we caught both bass and pickerel in the drop-offs adjacent to flats by using soft-plastic jerkbaits. We targeted the flats closest to the river channel and worked Case Salty Shads on a weighted flutter hook in depths up to 20 feet. We not only came home with some nice fish that day, but also saw two beautiful bald eagles, a black bear, and numerous deer as well.

Boats can be launched at one of the following ramps on Lake Moomaw: Fortney Branch at the southern end, Coles Point on the eastern side, and Bolar Flat on the western bank. Parking costs $5 from May 1 through October 1. *Note:* No boats over 25 feet in length are permitted on the lake. For lake information, go to www.fishonlakemoomaw.com.

BIG FISH TIP *To fish the standing timber in the coves and creeks of the lake, try a "drop-shot" with Case Magic Stiks in the June Bug color.*

Maury River (Rockbridge County)

The history-rich Maury River begins near Goshen where the Calfpasture and the Little Calfpasture rivers meet, just west of Goshen Pass. This gorgelike, high-gradient part of the Maury, with the qualities of a great trout stream (as discussed in chapter 2, pp. 29–30), is stocked by the Virginia Department of Game and Inland Fisheries in the stretch that passes through Goshen–Little North Mountain

Maury River, near Goshen

Wildlife Management Area. The WMA allows public access to the river through much of Goshen Pass, where it can be wade fished if water levels are low. Below here, canoeists and fishermen will find excellent floating opportunities from Rockbridge Baths to the Maury's confluence with the James River at Glasgow. Two small dams presently impound the river—one at Lexington and the other near Buena Vista—where you'll find both species of black bass as well as redbreast sunfish.

When fishing the Maury, work the ends of pools above its numerous rapids, timber and logjams, deep water ledges, and current breaks behind boulders. Spin fishermen may want to "gear down" to ultralight tackle for the shallow, clear pools on this steam, where both smallmouth and rock bass reside. I suggest using a 4-pound test line on a 5- to 6-foot rod. Small spinners, 3-inch Rapalas, Tiny Torpedos, and plastic jigs will cover just about all angling situations from swift riffles to slow, deep pools to shoreline cover. Try Clousers, Murray's Hellgrammites, poppers, and Kreel Clawdad patterns on a fly-rod. Smallmouth bass, rock bass, and redbreast sunfish are in abundance, making for an exciting day of fly-fishing action.

The following list of float trips includes locations of, and distances between, all the public landings on the Maury River. *Note:* You can estimate travel time for fishing at approximately 1 mile per hour. CAUTION: The Maury River above Rockbridge Baths (Goshen Pass) along VA 39 is not fishable by open canoe; this is a whitewater area with Class IV rapids. For stream classifications of rapids, see the list on pp. xiii–xiv.

Rockbridge Baths (Maury General Store on VA 39 and informal pull-offs along VA 602) **to Alone Mill** (informal pull-off along VA 622)

DISTANCE: 8 miles

VIRGINIA ATLAS AND GAZETTEER: 53

DIRECTIONS: (1) *Put-in at Rockbridge Baths.* From I-64 near Lexington, take exit 55 to U.S. 11 north. Turn left onto VA 39 west and travel 12 miles to Rockbridge Baths. Informal launches are located near the old country store and post office on VA 39 and just below the bridge at informal pull-offs along VA 602. (2) *Take-out at Alone Mill.* The take-out—essentially a steep dirt path—is located at the VA 622 bridge (Alone Mill Road, off VA 39), where limited parking is available. To reach the take-out from I-64 at Lexington, take VA 39 west about 5 miles to VA 622 (Alone Mill Road) and turn left. *Note:* This trip is for experienced canoeists only.

While there is excellent angling on this section of the Maury, the challenge here is to hit the river at the right level (or flow) for fishing. In the spring, when water levels are conducive to floating, most of your time and effort will be spent negotiating the seemingly continuous Class II+ rapids you encounter. In the summer and fall, when water levels allow you to "work" the river at a reasonable rate, these same rapids turn into shallow rock fields and ledges that you must continuously walk and pull your vessel through and over. In either case, fishermen and -women will find it difficult to traverse this section of river, much less fish it! These concerns notwithstanding, this is an outstanding trip with spectacular scenery that includes steep cliffs and forested shoreline. Besides continuous Class II–III rapids, you'll come across numerous islands, rock gardens, and large boulders. *Note:* You will need to scout many of these rapids before attempting to run them and may choose to portage most along the shoreline, depending on the time of year, water levels, and your proficiency as a paddler. The take-out—steep dirt path—is on river left directly below the VA 622 bridge.

BIG FISH TIP *Secure your gear to your craft and leave your best rods at home for this trip in case you take a spill—and ALWAYS wear a life vest.*

Alone Mill (informal pull-off along VA 622) **to Bean's Bottom** (informal pull-off along VA 631) **to East Lexington Town Park/ Jordan's Point** (cement landing just off U.S 11)

DISTANCE: 5.5 miles to Bean's Bottom; 8 miles from Alone Mill to East Lexington Town Park/Jordan's Point

VIRGINIA ATLAS AND GAZETTEER: 53

DIRECTIONS: (1) *Put-in at Alone Mill.* To reach the put-in from I-64 at Lexington, take exit 55 onto U.S. 11 north. Turn left onto VA 39 west and go about 5 miles to VA 622 (Alone Mill Road) and turn left again. The launch is down a dirt path below the VA 622 bridge (Alone Mill Road, off VA 39). (2a) *Take-out at Bean's Bottom.* The first take-out is at the VA 631 bridge (Furrs Mills Road, off U.S. 11). To reach it from I-64 at Lexington, take U.S. 11 south into Lexington and turn right onto Furrs Mills Road and drive until you reach the bridge. (2b) *Take-out at East Lexington Town Park/Jordan's Point.* The second take-out is at East Lexington Town Park/Jordan's Point, just off U.S. 11 at a cement landing, upstream of Lexington Dam. To reach it from I-64 at Lexington, take U.S. 11 south for about 1 mile and make the first right after crossing the Maury River, thus entering the park.

You can expect to catch literally scores of smallmouth bass, redbreast sunfish, fallfish, and redeye on this trip. I have done so on several occasions using both spinning and fly-rods. Most of the fish will be small, under a pound, so ultralight tackle is best. On the first 2 to 3 miles of this trip a maze of small islands, emergent willow-grass beds, sloughs, small rapids, and cobblestone-filled pools create a veritable wader's paradise. In the summer months, when the water is low and gin-clear, wading is an effective way to fish these especial-

Nice smallmouth bass

ly promising-looking areas. At about the 4-mile point you will encounter Horse-shoe Bend—a long river-right curve with a small island at the bottom (and best passage on the right). A fabulous stretch of water lies below the island where numerous deep boulder fields await. About a mile before the first take-out you will pass under the I-64 bridge, below which an island sits with a Class II rapid that can be run on its left side. Scout first! The Bean's Bottom take-out is on river left at the Furrs Mills Road (VA 631) bridge. Try using small plastic jigs and 3-inch minnow plugs (such as Rapalas) on this float in the springtime, and in-line spinners, plastic flukes, and topwater plugs (such as Tiny Torpedos) in the summer and fall.

Shortly past Bean's Bottom, you will encounter a stretch of slow water with deep pools before reaching an island that can be run either through the middle at normal levels or to the left during low flow. Watch for debris if you attempt to run to the left. Following the island you will see a beautiful arched rock formation along the bluffs on river right. Just before this, Whistle Creek enters the river, creating a spectacular cascading waterfall that is not to be missed. Throughout this area you will encounter slow, languid pools with plenty of ledges and submerged boulders that provide excellent smallmouth habitat, and then come upon an old mill dam that forms a Class I rapid, below which a long rock wall on river left extends for several hundred yards and offers great fishing. Soon after the wall ends, you will see a pump station on river right, in front of which a "knee dam" extends completely across the river. This can be run in the middle if the water is up, but must be portaged on river left at low flow. Below this you'll feel the effects of the Lexington Dam at Jordan's Point and will have to paddle the remaining three-quarter-mile trip through a pond that is created by the backwater. The take-out is at the cement landing on river right just above the Lexington Dam at East Lexington Town Park/Jordan's Point. CAUTION: Do not miss the take-out or you will drop over a 10-foot dam that sits merely 40 feet downstream!

BIG FISH TIP *Fly-fisherman should find success working small poppers along the shoreline and streamers in the runs below rapids.*

East Lexington Town Park/Jordan's Point (gravel trail to river on U.S. 11) **to Ben Salem Wayside** (informal pull-offs on U.S. 60)

DISTANCE: 6 miles

VIRGINIA ATLAS AND GAZETTEER: 53

DIRECTIONS: (1) *Put in at East Lexington Town Park/Jordan's Point.* The launch is located below the Lexington Dam at East Lexington Town Park/Jordan's Point (just off U.S. 11). To reach it from I-64 at Lexington, take U.S. 11 south for about 1 mile and make the first right after crossing the Maury River, thus entering the park. Be prepared to carry your vessel about 50 yards to access the river. (2) *Take-out at Ben Salem Wayside.* The take-out is on U.S. 60, east of I-81 at Lexington. Take the U.S. 60 exit off of I-81 just east of Lexington. You'll need to carry your canoe up a short, steep embankment here.

This float includes Class I–II rapids, numerous riffles, water-willow beds, large islands, and small dam remnants. During the first half of the trip you will encounter scattered light rapids, some rock bluffs, and long still stretches of water that offer excellent popper action on the fly-rod for sunfish, rock bass, and small bass. At about the 2.5-mile point the stonework from an old dam and boat lock requires paddlers to make a hard right, then left. CAUTION: Do not attempt to run through the middle of the lock.

At the midway point, you will pass under the I-81 bridge, and find excellent smallmouth bass fishing for the next few miles. Long deep pools with ledges and boulders create ideal habitat between rapids. Soft-plastic baits, especially flukes, and topwater plugs such as Pop-Rs are very effective summer baits, while spinnerbaits and various 3-inch jerkbaits are good spring and fall lures to try here. This is a very scenic stretch where you'll likely see lots of wildlife, including deer, ducks, geese, beavers, muskrats, osprey, and bald eagles.

Past this part of the float you'll come across the remains of South River dam, a Class II rock garden that you can run on far right or walk your boat through on the left. The river gets shallow below here, and a couple of small islands follow that should be run on the left side. A mile below the remnants of the dam, prepare for a series of ledges that run diagonally across the river and create an extended Class I+ rapid. Ben Salem Wayside follows. The river-right take-out at the wayside avoids the dam downstream, above Buena Vista. To reach the take-out continue about a quarter mile farther downstream to the sign on river right. *Note:* When this book was written, the I-81 bridge was under construction and required a long portage along the Chessie Nature Trail on river left.

Glen Maury Park in Buena Vista (canoe slide off VA 745) **to Locher Landing in Glasgow** (gravel launch off VA 684)

DISTANCE: 12 miles

VIRGINIA ATLAS AND GAZETTEER: 53/54

DIRECTIONS: (1) *Put-in at Glen Maury Park.* The launch is off VA 745 (via VA 608 from U.S. 60). To reach it from I-81, take the U.S. 60 exit east of Lexington and follow the signs to the park. The ramp is a canoe slide, and the park provides parking, camping, and bathroom

facilities. (2) *Take-out at Locher Landing.* The take-out is off VA 684
(via VA 130 from Natural Bridge). To reach it from I-81, take the
Natural Bridge exit onto U.S. 11, then take VA 130 east to Glasgow
and turn right onto VA 684. This road ends at the landing. *Note:*
River Road (VA 663) provides informal take-outs midway through
the trip near the Kanawha Canal Locks and across the river from
a large quarry. CAUTION: There are numerous "blown" dams that
create Class I–III rapids, some of which must be portaged due to
impassability. During low water levels you will have to walk your
vessel down through rocks and concrete debris. The fishing can be
outstanding in the water both above and below these areas, however.

Fly-fishing on the Maury River

This is a phenomenal trip, where 100+fish days are a possibility during the summer months, as the smallmouth bass habitat is incredible throughout most of the float. Rapids followed by long deep pools filled with chunk rock and ledges make up the first couple of miles or so, offering excellent angling opportunities. Fish the tops of the pools in the rapids, then the rocky shoreline until you reach the "pushwater" back of the pools, and work this area by casting far in front of your craft. I suggest using a soft-plastic of some sort (such as a curly tail grub or fluke) to fish the rapids and pushwater, and a topwater plug (like a Tiny Torpedo or Pop-R) to work along the shoreline. CAUTION: At the second rapid (about a mile into the trip), you'll encounter a wicked strainer created by overhanging trees on river right. Stay left and walk your boat or canoe through the rapid if necessary. Soon you will pass under a railroad trestle that crosses a large pool with great fly-fishing opportunities for bass and bream on poppers.

At about the 3-mile point, you will come to several islands and the remains of an old dam with a 2-foot drop. Take the channel to the far left or portage through the chute on the right; do not attempt to run this rapid through the center! Past the islands are two fantastic ledges that morph into Class II rapids when the water is high; run these to the right, or wade fish them when the water is low. Below here is a long pool and rocky beach on river left that is a good stopping point. Characterized by a series of elongated midriver ledges, this is a true "big fish" section of the Maury. I have caught numerous quality smallmouth in this area, including a citation-class fish the succumbed to a Case Salty Shad in July 2005, while I was canvassing the floats discussed in this chapter.

At the 4.5-mile point of this junket, the remains of Goose Neck Dam create a Class III rapid. There is no safe route here, so be sure to land on the bank and scout. I suggest that you walk your canoe through this rapid on river right when the water is low. Below here are the longest rapids of the trip—Class I water builds into a Class II wavefield, followed by back-to-back Class II+ ledges that end in a significant drop. Take the first part to the left, then run the last ledge in the center. Another dam site follows that can be run through the center when the water is high, but watch for pourover rocks. This can also be portaged through the chute on river left at low water levels.

The next mile or so offers outstanding smallmouth habitat, to where Buffalo Creek enters on river right (at the 7-mile point). Grass beds, shallow ledges, and rocky shoreline all hold feisty small-mouth by the hundreds. Just below the mouth of Buffalo Creek is one of the trickiest spots on the river. The current in the main chan-nel pushes boats right into large overhanging trees and their roots. The safest course is to walk your canoe through here. Soon you will see the rock quarry on river right. The bend here sits approxi-mately 3 miles before the take-out. Near the end of the trip you will pass under an old iron bridge frame that marks the float's 11-mile point. Begin scouting for Locher Landing, which you will reach a mile farther on river right just above a railroad bridge and before a serious Class III rapid that sits upstream of where the Maury enters the James. *Note:* Do not miss the take-out, or you will be dumped into the James River. You will have to carry your canoe up a steep embankment here.

BIG FISH TIP *Case Salty Shads are deadly for summertime smallies on the lower Maury.*

4

Fishing South Holston Lake and the North Fork of the Holston River

The North, Middle, and South forks of the Holston River eventually end their journeys through the mountains of southwest Virginia in the state of Tennessee, with the Middle and South forks impounded to form South Holston Lake, the largest reservoir in the far southwest part of the Old Dominion. Because of this, these two tributaries experience annual spring spawning runs of both walleye and white bass. In fact, there is a resident walleye population in the South Fork up to Damascus. Furthermore, the upper reaches of these two streams are also stocked with trout, while the North Fork is not. Nonetheless, while all three tributaries offer good smallmouth bass fishing, only the bronzeback fishery on the North Fork is exceptional. In fact, the North Fork is designated as "trophy" smallmouth bass water from the Loretta Norris bridge (VA 634) in Saltville downstream to the Tennessee state line. All fish under 20 inches must be released, and only 1 smallmouth larger than that may be kept per angler per day. While this section of the river is considered navigable, it is often prone to low water levels in the summer, and certain junkets may require some portaging. *Note:* The North Fork below Saltville is under a health advisory due to mercury contamination, and fish caught there should not be consumed.

South Holston Lake

VIRGINIA ATLAS AND GAZETTEER: 22

DIRECTIONS: To access the Whitaker Hollow ramp, take exit 19 off I-81 and follow U.S. 58 east to VA 722, then follow the public boat launch signs to the landing. To access all other public ramps, take VA 75 south (I-81, exit 17) toward the lake and follow the public boat landing signs.

South Holston Lake in Washington County extends southward into northeastern Tennessee, with most of the 7,580-acre impoundment located in our neighboring state and controlled by the Tennessee Valley Authority. Fantastic angling for both smallmouth and largemouth bass can be found here, and the lake also supports a healthy rainbow trout population (6-fish creel limit, 7-inch minimum size). There is no size limit for black bass on the lake, but statewide creel limits of 5 fish per day apply.

Butch Neal, owner of Neal's Handcrafted Lures in Abingdon, Virginia, recommends using Duck Flies and spoons in winter for smallmouth bass. In "float-and-fly," the traditional cold-water tactic practiced throughout far southwestern Virginia, an angler uses a crappie jig, float, and a long 10-foot rod to suspend the fly off the bottom and jig it, like one might work a spoon. As per its name, the

South Holston Lake

fly is usually made from duck feathers, though other materials can be used. To employ this technique, target lake points and use the depth finder to locate schools of baitfish, then adjust the float to set the fly down to that level.

Great walleye fishing is also reported on the lake, which is stocked annually, with a 5-fish, 18-inch minimum size limit. Many anglers target walleye by trolling deep-running minnow plugs and worm harnesses across points and drop-offs at night during the summer months. I find a deer-hair jig effective, tipped with a minnow to locate deep schools of fish during the winter. In the spring, walleye can be found in the shallower regions at the upper end of the lake, and make a spawning run in the South and Middle forks of the Holston. You'll find the best fishing above the Avens Ramp on located on VA 672. Follow the public boat landing signs off VA 75, south of Abingdon.

Anglers can also launch boats at Washington County Park near the Tennessee state line (off VA 664, fee required), at the Sportsman's Marina (also off VA 664, fee required) and at Whitaker Hollow (near the lake's headwaters on its southern shoreline). *Note:* South Holston Lake experiences a 20-foot winter drawdown controlled by the Tennessee Valley Authority every year, making some ramps unusable.

North Fork of the Holston River

The fishery on this once overlooked river has rebounded exceptionally from the pollution problems it experience a few decades ago.

Redbreast sunfish, channel catfish, and rock bass can be found here in abundance, and smallmouth bass ranging from 3 to 4 pounds are common. The North Fork is difficult to access, however, due to the lack of public boat landings. Some launches are informal pull-offs at bridge crossings or on private property along VA 611, so be sure to obtain permission if you wish to use these. *Note:* Low water levels during the summer months may require boaters to pull vessels across shallow ledges in some places.

My favorite time to fish the North Fork of the Holston is during the spring, when the water is high. One of my go-to lures on such trips is a simple Fat Albert Grub, rigged on a ⅛-ounce jig head. Other plastics, such as lizards, tubes, and flukes, will also work well. Summer trips on the North Fork call for topwater baits such as Pop-Rs and Tiny Torpedos; search out the ends of deeper pools with riffles above to work these lures. When the water is low, I prefer to pull the canoe aside before entering and wading into promising areas such as these. Another summer favorite here is a buzzbait, which can be cast from the middle of this stream to either bank in many places,

Bass fishing

allowing for full coverage of the water. The fine, top topwater action on the North Fork continues well into the fall during most years. In the winter months, anglers generally drift the slower sections of the river, employing the "float-and-fly" method of fishing described earlier. For fly-fishing, I suggest using any variety of hellgrammite or crayfish pattern in the riffles, and poppers along the bank.

The following list of float trips includes locations of, and distances between, all the public accesses on the North Fork of the Holston River in Washington County above U.S. 19. Unfortunately, no public access exists below this point (as of the writing of this book). Most landings are informal unless otherwise noted. *Note:* You can estimate travel time for fishing at approximately 1 mile per hour. For stream classifications of rapids, see the list on pp. xiii–xiv.

Rich Valley Show Grounds (informal pull-off at VA 630 bridge) to North Holston (informal pull-off on VA 91)

DISTANCE: 7 miles

VIRGINIA ATLAS AND GAZETTEER: 22

DIRECTIONS: (1) *Put-in at Rich Valley Show Grounds.* From I-81, at exit 35 (Saltville/Chilhowie), take VA 107 north to Saltville and turn right onto VA 91 (East Main Street). Follow this road for about 10 miles to VA 630 and turn right. The launch is at an informal pull-off at the VA 630 bridge (Long Hollow Road). *Note:* Access is difficult here, but the nearby school grounds may allow for limited weekend parking. (2) *Take-out at North Holston.* From I-81, at exit 35 (Saltville/Chilhowie), take VA 107 north to Saltville and turn right onto

VA 91 (East Main Street). Go about 5 miles. The take-out is at an informal pull-off along VA 91 near the town of North Holston, just west of VA 633 (Possum Hollow Road).

This stretch of the North Fork runs through pastoral farmland, with a few deep pools and shallow gravel flats that make for good spring canoe or kayak fishing. It can also be fished effectively by wading and using small plastic grubs or flukes or live hellgrammites in the summertime. *Note:* Due to the extremely shallow areas on this stretch, I suggest making this trip only during periods of high water flow in spring. The informal take-out is on river right in a big bend along VA 91.

North Holston (informal pull-off on VA 91) **to Saltville public boat landing** (concrete ramp in Saltville)

DISTANCE: 4 miles

VIRGINIA ATLAS AND GAZETTEER: 22

DIRECTIONS: (1) *Put-in at North Holston.* From I-81, at exit 35 (Saltville/Chilhowie), take VA 107 north to Saltville and turn right onto VA 91 (East Main Street). Go about 5 miles. The launch is at an informal pull-off along VA 91 near the town of North Holston, just west of VA 633 (Possum Hollow Road). (2) *Take-out at Saltville public boat landing.* From I-81, at exit 35 (Saltville/Chilhowie), take VA 107 north to Saltville and turn right onto VA 91 (East Main Street). Then turn left at the sign for the Saltville public boat landing onto Government Plant Road, and continue to follow the signs until you reach the concrete ramp.

This section of the river includes three very deep mining holes (which go down 25 feet in some places), and a variety of rocky pools and wood cover make for both good winter and summer fishing areas. I suggest working the deep holes as slowly as possible during both seasons with ¼-ounce tube jigs and plastic grubs or jig-and-pigs. *Note:* Due to the extremely shallow stretches on this float, I suggest making this trip only during periods of high water flow in spring. The take-out is on river left, at the concrete landing in Saltville.

Saltville public boat landing (concrete ramp in Saltville) to Virginia Department of Game and Inland Fisheries property (concrete ramp on VA 611, at "40 acre field")

DISTANCE: 6 miles

VIRGINIA ATLAS AND GAZETTEER: 22

DIRECTIONS: (1) *Put-in at Saltville public boat landing.* From I-81, at exit 35 (Saltville/Chilhowie), take VA 107 north to Saltville and turn right onto VA 91 (East Main Street). Then turn left at the sign for the Saltville public boat landing onto Government Plant Road, and continue to follow the signs until you reach the concrete ramp. (2) *Take-out at VDGIF property.* From I-81, at exit 35 (Saltville/Chilhowie), take VA 107 north to Saltville and turn left onto VA 91 (Main Street), then turn right onto Allison Gap Road (VA 634). Immediately turn left again onto VA 611. The landing is located a few miles down this road on the Virginia Department of Game and Inland Fisheries property (known locally as "40 acre field"). CAUTION: The gradient of the river increases sharply downstream of

Saltville. There is a particularly tricky Class III rapid below the Lo-retta Norris bridge (VA 643) that will push you against a rock wall on river right at certain water levels (see below).

This float offers beautiful scenery, river bluffs, riffles, and pocket water, and the section downstream of the Olin Plant is especially known for big fish. While this trip offers excellent fishing, it can sometimes prove treacherous, and there are a number of places where you should exercise caution. The first is at the first bridge you encounter, at Government Plant Road. This Class I rapid is not particularly bad, but it may prove hard to pass through at low water levels, and you can easily scout and walk it. The second is an old dam about half a mile below the bridge. Here, the water flows to river right around the dam, making a very sharp turn where you'll encounter scattered rocks; if possible, you should pull up on the dam and scout before running it. The third is at the Loretta Norris bridge, about half a mile below the aforementioned dam, where a Class II rapid is formed by very large rocks and a narrow chute on river left. You should scout this thoroughly before running it, and walk your vessel through it in places if need be. The fourth is the worst rapid on this trip and lies about three quarters of a mile below the Loretta Norris bridge. Here you'll encounter a big white wall of earth on river right and a cliff on river left where huge boulders loom 15 to 20 feet high. The rapid begins about 50 yards below. CAUTION: There is a 4-foot drop-off here, with narrow chutes and very large rocks. At normal flows, this is a Class III rapid, but it can morph into a Class IV when the water is higher. You can run it on river right with a raft, but you may need to portage smaller vessels. In the summer, the water will be low enough that you can get out on river right and check it out first. Below you'll find a great area to fish once you successfully navigate through this stretch. After this last rapid there are no major obstacles the rest of the way to the ramp. *Note:* This superb trip can be made by johnboat or raft only when the water levels are sufficiently high during the winter or spring months. The take-out is a concrete ramp on river right along VA 611 at the Virginia Department of Game and Inland Fisheries property.

BIG FISH TIP *Use ½-ounce Neal's spinnerbaits in the springtime when the water is high and dingy; these handmade lures were designed with this river in mind.*

Virginia Department of Game and Inland Fisheries property

(concrete ramp on VA 611, at "40 acre field") **to Big Falls** (informal pull-off along VA 611)

DISTANCE: 8 miles

VIRGINIA ATLAS AND GAZETTEER: 22

DIRECTIONS: (1) *Put-in at VDGIF property.* From I-81, at exit 35 (Saltville/Chilhowie), take VA 107 north to Saltville and turn left onto VA 91 (Main Street), then turn right onto Allison Gap Road (VA 634). Immediately turn left again onto VA 611. The landing is located a few miles down this road on the Virginia Department of Game and Inland Fisheries property (known locally as "40 acre field"). (2) *Take-out at Big Falls.* From I-81, follow the directions to the put-in and continue on VA 611 approximately 6 miles until you reach Big Falls. The informal, roadside take-out is on VA 611, below Big Falls.

This is an isolated trek with great fishing opportunities along the scattered ledges, riffles, and bluff banks. *Note:* Though numerous Class II+ rapids on this stretch of the North Fork, especially below where Big Tumbling Creek enters on river right, make this an arduous trip, the runs created by these rapids provide excellent angling opportunities during the summer months. I like to stop and wade these areas with the fly-rod, using various "creature patterns" such as Crystal Buggers or Murray's Hellgrammites. CAUTION: At Big Falls (Class III), the river widens to become a series of elongated shelves running parallel to each other down the middle. I suggest that you take one of the many rocky chutes along the river's left side and walk your craft through this shallower region. The river-right take-out (an informal pull-off) is directly below Big Falls.

BIG FISH TIP *Use large topwater plugs or buzzbaits on cloudy days here to catch big smallies.*

Big Falls (informal pull-off along VA 611) **to VA 80 bridge** (informal pull-off along VA 611)
DISTANCE: 4 miles
VIRGINIA ATLAS AND GAZETTEER: 22
DIRECTIONS: (1) *Put-in at Big Falls.* From I-81, at exit 35 (Saltville/Chilhowie), take VA 107 north to Saltville and turn left onto VA 91 (East Main Street), then immediately turn right onto Allison Gap

Road (VA 634). Turn left again onto VA 611 and travel about 10 miles. The launch is below Big Falls, on VA 611. (2) *Take-out at VA 80 bridge.* From the launch, continue down VA 611 to the intersection with VA 80; you'll find places to park on the left. *Alternative route to take-out.* From I-81 at the Meadowview/VA 80 exit, take VA 80 north until you reach the VA 80 bridge; the take-out is on its north side, on the right.

This junket lacks major rapids, but sandbars and big islands allow for good prespawn angling. You'll want to begin by fishing the excellent water below the falls, which can be especially productive in the early spring before there is too much fishing pressure. As you start down the river you will need to take the left chute around the large island that sits below the falls. Once you clear the island, the terrain is a pretty constant combination of long pools below riffles, submerged ledges, and grass beds. If you are spin fishing in the summer months, you will want to work these areas with Senkos, Jack's Worms, and various topwater plugs; all of these lures have produced quality fish for me here. I've also found that Chernobyl Ants/Hoppers drifted along the banks work well for taking smallmouth and sunfish on the fly-rod. The take-out is along a dirt bank on river right, just before the VA 80 bridge, where Wolf Creek enters the river. *Note:* Riverside Church Road may also allow access during the week.

BIG FISH TIP *Creek mouths are invariable hotspots for summer smallies; my wife, Beth, once caught a bass in excess of 2 pounds on the fly-rod at the mouth of Wolf Creek.*

VA 80 bridge (informal pull-off along VA 611) **to U.S. 19 bridge**
(very limited access along VA 611)

DISTANCE: 12 miles

VIRGINIA ATLAS AND GAZETTEER: 21/22

DIRECTIONS: (1) *Put-in at VA 80 bridge.* From I-81 at the Mead-
owview/VA 80 exit, take VA 80 north until you reach the VA 80
bridge; the put-in is on its north side, on the right. (2) *Take-out at
U.S. 19 bridge.* From I-81, at Abingdon, take U.S. 11 (Main Street)
to VA 692 north (Whites Mill Road) to the Toole Creek bridge, then
take VA 611 south to the U.S. 19 bridge. The take-out is on river
right. *Note:* U.S. 19 can also be reached via I-81 at Abingdon; however, at the time this book was written, the U.S. 19 bridge was under
construction and access to the river was limited.

This trip offers some great fishing, including a good mix of riffles,
long pools, and pocket water. You'll find good places for wade fishing along North Fork River Road (VA 611), at numerous pull-offs
between the put-in and take-out points, including some areas where
river fords exist. Some informal pull-offs along VA 611, just downstream of VA 687, can also serve as alternative launch or exit points.
Keep in mind that landowner permission may be required.

BIG FISH TIP *Fish live hellgrammites in the riffles and crayfish in the deeper
holes. A super summer bait for North Fork smallies is a Texas-rigged Case
Magic Stik.*

Appendix: Information and Resources

Camping

Bolar Mountain Recreation Area
Warm Springs Ranger District
Route 2, Box 30
Hot Springs, VA 24445
(540) 839-2521
www.fs.fed.us/r8/gwj/warmsprings/recreation/day_use_areas/
bolar_mountain_rec_area.shtml

Clinch Mountain Wildlife Management Area
Route 2
Marion, VA 24370
(276) 944-5024
www.dgif.state.va.us/hunting/wma/clinch_mountain.html

George Washington (and Jefferson) National Forests
5162 Valleypointe Parkway
Roanoke, VA 24019
(540) 962-2214
www.fs.fed.us/r8/gwj/

Warm Springs District
Route 2, Box 30
Hot Springs, VA 24445
(540) 839-2521
www.fs.fed.us/r8/gwj/warmsprings/

Grayson Highlands State Park
829 Grayson Highland Lane
Mouth of Wilson, VA 24363
(276) 579-7092 or 1-(800) 933-PARK
www.dcr.state.va.us/parks/graysonh.htm

Mount Rogers National Recreation Area
3714 Highway 16
Marion, VA 24354
(276) 783-5196 or 1-(800) 628-7202
www.fs.fed.us/r8/gwj/mr/

Riverside Campground
18469 North Fork River Road
Abingdon, VA 24210
(276) 628-5333
www.holidayjunction.com/usa/va/cva0004.html

Fishing Regulations

Virginia Department of Game and Inland Fisheries
www.dgif.state.va.us (main VDGIF Web site)
Region III Office
1796 Highway Sixteen
Marion, VA 24354
(276) 783-4860

Region IV Office
127 Lee Highway
Verona, VA 24482
(540) 248-9360

Guides, Liveries, and Outfitters

Alleghany Highlands Guide Service
P.O. Box 9
Goodview, VA 24095
(540) 890-4653
www.fishonlakemoomaw.com

Alleghany Outfitters
The Homestead
P.O. Box 2000
Hot Springs, VA 24445
(540) 839-1760
www.thehomestead.com/outdoor-activities.asp

Blue Blaze Bike and Shuttle Service
226 W. Laurel Avenue
Damascus, VA, 24236
(276) 475-5095 or 1-(800) 475-5095
www.blueblazebikeandshuttle.com
blueblaze@naxs.com

Blue Ridge Fly Fishers
5524 Williamson Road
Suite 20
Roanoke, VA 24012
(540) 563-1617
www.blueridgeflyfishers.com

Elk Creek Outfitters
1560 Highway 105
Boone, NC 28607
(828) 264-6497
www.ecoflyfishing.com

Greasy Creek Outfitters
P.O. Box 211
Willis, VA 24380
(540) 789-7811
www.greasycreekoutfitters.com

Llewellyn Lodge Outdoors
603 S. Main Street
Lexington, VA 24450
(540) 463-3235 or 1-(800) 882-1145
www.vatrout.com

Reel Time Fly Fishing
23 W. Washington Street
Lexington, VA 24450
(540) 462-6100

Twin River Outfitters
917 Rockbridge Road
Glasgow, VA 24555
(540) 258-1999
www.canoevirginia.net

Virginia Creeper Fly-fishing
16501 JEB Stuart Highway
Abingdon, VA, 24211
(276) 628-3826
www.vcflyshop.com

Virginia Highlands Fly Fishing
P.O. Box 372
Monterey, VA 24465
(540) 468-2395
www.geocities.com/finsandfeathers2003

Lodging/Dining Information

Abingdon Convention and Visitors Bureau
335 Cummings Street
Abingdon, VA 24210
(276) 676-2282 or 1-(800) 435-3440
www.abingdon.com

Blue Ridge Travel Association
Regional Visitor's Center
975 Tazewell Street
Wytheville, VA 24382
1-(800) 446-9670
www.virginiablueridge.org

Highland County Chamber of Commerce
P.O. Box 223
Monterey, VA 24465
(540) 468-2550
www.highlandcounty.org

Maps

DeLorme's Virginia Atlas and Gazetteer, 6th edition, (Yarmouth, Maine: DeLorme, 2005). ISBN 0-89933-326-5. Widely available at bookstores and online sources, or see www.delorme.com (DeLorme, Two DeLorme Drive, P.O. Box 298, Yarmouth, ME 04096, 1-(800) 561-5105) for information

The Maury River Atlas, by Wm. E. Trout III. Available from the Virginia Canals and Navigations Society, 6826 Rosemont Drive, McLean, VA 22101 http://organizations.rockbridge.net/canal/ default.htm (see the link for VC&NS publications)

Twin River Outfitters
917 Rockbridge Road
Glasgow, VA 24555
(540) 261-7334
www.canoevirginia.net

Parks

Bolar Mountain Recreation Area
Warm Springs Ranger District
Route 2, Box 30
Hot Springs, VA 24445
(540) 839-2521
www.fs.fed.us/r8/gwj/warmsprings/recreation/day_use_areas/
bolar_mountain_rec_area.shtml

Grayson Highlands State Park
289 Grayson Highland Lane
Mouth of Wilson, VA 24363
(276) 579-7092 or 1-(800) 933-PARK
www.dcr.state.va.us/parks/graysonh.htm

Mount Rogers National Recreation Area
3714 Highway 16
Marion, VA 24354
(276) 783-5196 or 1-(800) 628-7202
www.fs.fed.us/r8/gwj/mr/

Tackle Shops
The Bait Place
707 E. Morris Hill Road
Covington, VA 24426
(540) 965-0633

Lake Moomaw Marina
Bolar's Draft Road
Warm Springs, VA 24484
(540) 279-4144

Pro Bass Outdoors Shop
1099 Cummings Street
Abingdon, VA, 24211
(276) 619-5011

Index

Boldfaced page numbers refer to illustrations.